T0359563

Wakefield Press

Noticing

Jan Andrews grew up in Melbourne and studied there and in Boston. Teaching was followed by a career in public policy and administration. A lifelong engagement with language and poetry accompanied these travels. *Noticing* presents a selection of her poems.

Noticing

JAN ANDREWS

**Wakefield
Press**

Wakefield Press
16 Rose Street
Mile End
South Australia 5031
www.wakefieldpress.com.au

First published 2024

Designed and typeset by Michael Deves

ISBN 978 1 92304 248 3

A catalogue record for this book is available from the National Library of Australia

Wakefield Press thanks Coriole Vineyards for continued support

NOTICING

A selection of poems written across years.
The encouragement of friends made this possible
and to them my thanks.

Contents

BIRDWORDS

MISCHIEF

OLD

NOW-ISH

YOUNG

THE EARLY WORD CATCHES THE YEARN ...

In my childhood home –
leaf years pass outside my window;
words calling to me.

THE BLACK BOX OF SUMMER, 1960

Water in, cool air out,
Mr Carrier's invention worked a magic

on a wheeled, wire tower in the living room,
about head height if you were eight.

With walnut veneer in 'wipe-clean' plastic,
and louvres that only adults might direct,

it seemed a model of a house with shutters
from some hot and distant country,

or a Tibetan monastery square atop a mountain,
as pictured in the Atlas of the World and its Peoples.

Buckets were carried to it from the laundry,
unsettling, that volume of water brought inside.

Great care was taken not to spill it on the carpet,
Hi-Lo Autumn-Gold that matched the corgi.

Too loud to have on during the Graham Kennedy show,
and too costly to leave on overnight.

I wanted little ribbons to fly from the grille,
but this was regarded as bad taste.

CHARTRES

In this cool place the tall stone recommends
the particular rigour of its soft reflectiveness and clear lines.
Around the glass it quietly shapes a sufficient grace;
no flamboyant gothic here.

High up the blue glass sanctions imagination,
with evanescent colour.
No reason but the chance fall of light,
in the passing of the seasons, good weather and bad.

Perhaps in all the years there has never been one pattern quite
  the same;
for always the light dissolves the vaults,
and these faint ribs define the light;
but always they concur.

To stare only at blue glass discounts this fine agreement.
In some shifting facets of the haze
that fall across the floor,
appears this discipline of the insubstantial.

TRAVELLING EAST IN THE MORNING

Travelling east in the morning,
except where the tracks veer
around the river.
Sun on the cracked leather seat,
a still patch of warmth
near the old train's open door.
The rectangle frames
rapid patterns of light and dark,
flickering visions
of a fragile autumn world
about to break.
High blue sky stretches to paleness,
and a wind comes from hunting clouds in the south,
ice-edged, to lift sap-thin leaves
translucent to the light.
A sense of the world outside shifting uneasily,
edging to be off.
Leaves and birds' wings slip into fragments
and dissolve in the cold stream of wind.

Quickly, before the pool of sun disappears,
in the turn into the station,
before the door is blacked over by shadow,
in the back of the mind,
somewhere far outside this long moving tunnel,
is an ancient memory, of restlessness.

BOSTON

NIGHTMARE

About being in a cottage somewhere,
somewhere that was supposed to be safe,
as a 'cottage' ought to be.
Outside, a man hoed secure looking rows.
A bank, covered in brush.
Something moving out there, sort of often.
Sense of unease.
Sees a small animal,
possum, stray dog,
but feels much bigger,
a shape smutted from burrowing underground.
It moves behind the leaves
and lines of undergrowth, so never sure.
Tells the man, who moves further away.
Becomes nervous and locks the doors and windows.
Doesn't go out the back way, or at dusk at all.
But forgets the slate slab floor, and one night
the burrower comes up, big and looming.
A dusty shabby shape,
immovable, here inside the cottage.

STEP ON GRASS

The trouble today is
that roads all go somewhere,
neatly reach their ends,
map the land.

But what of roads that stop?
The purposeful footpaths of country towns
past their prime,
their wash of concrete
tossing like ice floes over tree roots.

Or the mistake in planning,
and the sequestered sweep –
to nothing
but the strange twittering of grass stalks.

Or those old Roman roads,
their deep flags engraving an empire's direction;
it's said that nothing grows in the cracks,
so surely were the stones cut.

What a surprise then
for the last row to encounter turf.
Step on grass and feel the choices.

ANTIQUE DISPOSITION

A sense of being the outsider;
I could break this plate.
The shock in the shop would be tremendous.
'A tall, seemingly calm, woman –
ah, but her eye was wild,
and wasn't she gaunt?'
just walked in,
smashed things.

Small crisp shards of blue-edged china
on the vacuumed carpet,
that clean underwriting of the studied clutter.
'Don't worry, it's alright.
The pieces can be disposed of,
just a plate gone,
a chip here.'

The past is manageable.
It can all be reduced
to a sweep of the rug.
The neat presumption of smooth shiny plates,
selling a lying cohesion,
delicate fluted things to pay the way of this hawker of past lives.
Ah, that's better; dust and chalky edges,
triangular bits,
faint floral complaints at the anonymising of it all.

WALL

There is a wall over which the ivy grows
and against which Christmas trees lean in their time.
Pleasing, the small bricks
coming together.

Against it the seasons of life display.
Spring suggests to the cords of creeper
quickness and a lacy exploration.
In December bareness –
pine crisp excitement in the tree market,
and whispering echoes of the wall's argument
in the snow tracery of mortar lines.
In summer, almost forgotten, it supports
shining leaves, and the bare-shouldered confidence
of those in the sun on the terrace.

But always the wall.
The lace, festivity and basking,
just curtains against the underlying certainty.
A known acceptance of interlocking pieces,
the quiet satisfaction of the basic pattern.

Come Fall all is seen.

BRING BACK DOROTHEA MACKELLAR, 1980

After the predictable stuff about animals –
'We saw the koala enclosure at the San Diego zoo.
They were so cute! I've always liked Australians, they're so
    friendly.'

   On with the diplomatic immunity then,
   and in for a long session.

***

'Your films are really good.
I saw the one about the schoolgirls in white dresses. Did you
    wear...?'

   No, I wore a grey uniform. 'Oh was that to keep the desert
   from marking your clothes?' Well, no, I lived in the city
   and mostly all school uniforms were grey. Well, the blazers
   weren't...' But didn't you find those long dresses, I mean
   even if they were grey, cumbersome?'

***

'You have a big white building
sort of with wings, don't you?'
'And the "outback", what's it really like?
Tough huh?'
'Do your kangaroos really box?'
'... and the one about the English
defeating you in a war.

But weren't you allies?'

Yes, we were. The film made it look like that because it was
making a statement about our relationship with England.
'Oh, so the war didn't really happen?'
'No, the war happened but through it we are said to have found
a sense of independence. 'Oh, like our war
of independence!' Well, in a sense like that, but ...
'But I thought you were allies?'

FLOTSAM

The homeless man sleeps now
in a pool of sun on the bench,
like a tattered script of seaweed
beached at high tide.
He turned his back to these high windows
to face the small lawn and the bushes
between the library and the street.
He pulled his face down
tight to his chest, and hutched his winter coat
against more than the cold.
He can see,
if he opens his eyes,
a thick segment of hedge
and the lower limbs of a wiry winter tree.
The angle is exact to see these things,
and he has found it in half an hour
of small shiftings of his head
on his newspaper pillow,
until, satisfied, he rests.

My guess is that the city planners
built these stretches of grass, shrub and bench
in clear perspectives to contain the natural order,
and people such as him.
But they underestimated the myriad forests
to be found in a hedge,
and the need for privacy.

ROUND POND, MAINE

For Elizabeth Sallies

After 'Upon Appleton House to my Lord Fairfax', Andrew Marvell, 1651

I

Round Pond. Named for its shape
and leaving unspoken
the luminous dark green of its shadows,
crossed in the depths by pale veins of water-buried birches,
older lines of beaver work cured to black in the preserving stillness,
and flecked brown trout moving confidently in this unfished place.

Large turtles amble their aquatic paths,
leathery necks turning in slow reaches
as if they judged something important.
Occasionally they broach the surface,
streams sluicing from their window-paned backs,
they turn back down again as if they had confirmed a choice.

Woven with bright shafts of otters
in tumbling quick pursuit,
silver nets of bubbles behind them.
Audacious knots of sleek brown bodies
pause to bask limpid in the sun
before the next deft descent to joy.

II

Round Pond. You walk its edge and streamers of alarmed frogs
hurl themselves into the water, to stare reproachfully,
their heads odd buds among the lily pads.
At dusk, great yellow throats ballooning, they will honk,
cough like sputtering motors,
plunk like flat banjo notes, and bellow like strange cattle.

Blue flag iris stretch out their small canopies,
pieced together in stitches
of sapphire dragonflies,
and darned into tiny blue hazes
by minute hummingbirds
until a piece of sky billows at the foot of the bank.

The wind fetches cloths of silver
from the water to pool into a corner bay,
and a roe deer lifts her head
at each new crinkling of light.

III

Round Pond. Rowing past the beaver dam
we surprise a sunning ribbon snake
into a magnificent scything leap,
a three-foot arc from the heap of willow branches
silently into the pool below,
like an old silver chain into a velvet bag.

Rocks bleached white by lichen frosts
foreshadow the heaping snows
that will quiet the woodchuck and chipmunk,
the goldfinch and woodpecker,
raccoon and goose, moose and bear,
and the fine, glittering lizard.

The woods rise straight from the shore.
Birch and aspen thread and serry
the clouds of ash and maple leaves.
The summer's fullness is fragile in New England.

IV

Round Pond. In the sweep of the clearing
stand the buildings made by those before you.
The Big House, the Guest House, the boatshed
were built with great care,
like the home-made presents of children, wrapped in white tissue
and tied in green or red, taut with the effort to get it right.

Inside, each room unwraps to a lining of old pine.
In the morning this seasoned richness
is diluted by the slicing air
to the colour of late afternoon light,
as if by a trick to remind you as you leave
of the warm inclusion of coming home.

At night, burnished by the fire's light
to a ruddy flicker,
it is as if all the squirrel tails and fox backs
have come home to these rooms,
red burr and sheen moving deep within the old varnish.

Such things are treasured in years to come,
for their simple grace and care,
unspoiled confidence,
a gift of innocence.

BRUNSWICK

CHAMELEON

Chameleon in winter, stone grey and brown,
carefully tracking the known runnels of sunlight between the
    great cold rocks,
warming to ochre and umber, stilling under clouds to mottled
    ash and dun,
hiding very well its true self against the vicissitudes of the sun.

AUTUMN SUNRISE

Behind the dark serrations
of the tall pines that edge the valley,
the sun lifts.
It lights the tops of autumn trees,
and illuminates the clouds of mist below
that together wash this landscape
of small cottages and parallel streets
with a chasing of flame and silver.

A girl with corn-gold hair,
thick-braided like some medieval figure,
steps through shadow and light in the street below,
her dark coat held tight around her,
collar raised against the cold.
Unmindful of the bright rich weaving of her hair,
a mirror to the glancing light,
she walks briskly to her day.

The elderly emerge
and make purposeful actions over small things,
as if to rationalise their chronic early rising.
Scooping into the shell-space of their rounded shoulders
and careful steps, the small preoccupations
of collecting a paper, putting out a bin,
or closing a gate.
Their stooped heads more thatches of grey.

What is it about the autumn light
that halves of things are made so bright
and the shadow side is made so clear
as the other half of what is dear?

ADELAIDE

SAFE HARBOUR

I lie curled around your back
like the pale crescent of sand half circling the bay,
holding the ebb and flow of our breath.

WISDOM AT THE GATE

With a week-old problem
still stuck in my head,
travel gives a surrogate sense of progress.

I drive down the ramp
into the usual carpark,
and wish there was a like solution to my thoughts.

Haul last night's papers from the boot
onto squeaking wheels,
of airport exact dimensions.

Tense the shoulders for the pull across the floor,
weave around someone's Harley,
all confidently resolved chrome shiny bits.

And there, cooped against the gate,
four hands high, and golden eyes,
a Boobook owl.

Soft feathers shirr,
shadow-rimpling chest,
warm leathered feet and holstered beak.

Then with no sound
he slips the strictures of the catacomb
and finds another way out.

WALKING THE POEM

Took a poem for a walk tonight.
It has sat grudgingly in the back of my mind,
like a cat ignoring you when you call.

I don't know yet how to set it free,
All I know is this weight
that's been sinking my spirit.

Last week in Singapore an execution,
office politics the week before,
last month more habitats destroyed,
many small animals lost and much beauty,
and the globe still warming up.
In July genocide in Africa, again,
another year of failing humanity on this small planet.

Turning into the park
from the channelling lines of streets
and cross-hatching moil of thoughts,
the broad green space
and pealing glory of evening light
take the tension out of my chest
in a long, slow unexpected exhalation.

And there in the early evening's blue-grey shadows,
in the deep dry creek bed beneath the footbridge,
sits a blue-grey Burmese on a flat blue-grey rock,
looking at me, tall, still and intent.

The poem has come out of my head. Not far –
it still sits shadowy and half subterranean in the culvert.
You know cats – they come in their own time, not yours.
It doesn't move. Appearing at all was the gift.

THE MASTECTOMY CHALLENGE CUP

On top of the prosthesis cabinet lie the saline implants.
Others spread less tidily,
lapping over each other on the green cloth,
with some starting up the wall
like an incoming tide of small pellucid jellyfish,
towards the 'Lips You'll Love' poster.
Inside the cabinet are the opaque pink ones
like shelled abalone.
'Hot New Mums' headlines the magazine pile.
The Teri Wipes box promises the quality of towelling in paper.
ProMed Latex glove boxes assure you of medical alliances.
I do not wish to enter this arena.

JASMINE CALLING

It's Jasmine from Newspoll
calling from Sydney
and she would like to speak
with the youngest member of the household
between the ages of 18 and 35.
That would be the dog, I say,
and there is a short, dense silence.

Probably just the time delay –
along the wire,
up to the satellites and back,
possibly between the post-coach stations,
or the pigeon's wing-beats,
or, just maybe, the generation gap
before a tense laugh and speedy retreat.

VENENUM REGINA

Poison queen, poison queen,
where are you tonight?

I'm out in the fields looking for the light.
Though I'm poison spun,
though my realm is black,
still I look for what I lack.

To unspin me, to redeem me,
to bring me back to life,
to unravel all the evil
I have woven into strife.

The nights are frightening for her
because the dark takes over hers.
By day her venom spreads,
at night, to her it turns.

Taught young that love could leave her,
she learned to leave it first,
by finding fault, then demeaning,
then despising, thence to kill.
This sad cycle sixty years repeating,
need imploding to vicious skill.

I'm sorry, but I cannot let you in,
for company and shelter excite your hate.
Others' trust you're driven to betray,
as yours was, so you must recreate.

But before you die come this way a little.
See this house, this window and its light,
spilling out across the fields,
breaking up the night.

IN 1938

For Flora Westley

Socks in progress, Dad's socks
were left out on the sideboard
to be added to in passing.
Their mother did the hard parts,
helped by visiting aunts over pots of tea,
but the girls learned well.
Flora, Vi and Jean could soon firm-edge
a double rib,
turn a heel and close a toe.
The well-to-do might purchase gentlemen's hosiery
in sleek silk blends;
working families knitted together.

AD HOC ADVICE

Hill of Content bookshop, March 20, 2014

This bit of small theatre must occur often.
'Where is the Post Office?'
    Not here.
    We've lost it.
Tempt their inner voices. Deep breath then.

To your right, out the door, across the road, on the diagonally
    opposite corner, once there you'll see the sign.

They look out the window. Don't trust 'once there'
Can't see it from this angle,
seek reassurance.
And because this is a bookshop
rather than the tailor or a restaurant,
they ask with the certainty they'll be answered.
Kindly.

ON THE GRAMMAR OF PUBLIC INSTRUCTIONS

FIRE EVACUATION:

Cease all activities.
>Breathing and walking excepted.
>Pack your fire
>in a small fire-proof box under your arm.

Vacate your area as quickly and safely as possible.
>If it's not possible
>just do your best.

Leave through nearest exit.
>That isn't a window.

Take a mobile phone.
>Anyone's will do.

When you have vacated the building,
>Or simply left it.

walk along the footpath,
>not the road,
>and never run or skip,

to the Assembly Point in front of the Town Houses.
>You will know these by their capitalised initials.

>Breathe regularly into the small opening of your fire-box;
>keep the flame alive.

GRIEF

It calls you to leave the house,
with its party going on
and people doing what they do.

You are called through the back door,
along a little-used track
to the bottom of the garden.

There an overgrown gate opens down
to a very long pathway
beneath the earth.

This path has many side rooms,
lit by faint lamps, or shadowy single bulbs
with sketchy wires to flickering generators.

All are dusty,
knotted with dry roots
and the barbed wire of desiccated ivy.

In some you stop to rest.
In others you search,
for something unclear.

In one you fight a battle from your bunker,
sniping at the outside
through a crack in the earthen wall.

In another you just sit for a long while,
gathering yourself.
There are many, many rooms.

Finally, the path opens into a hidden valley,
a deep cleft with a pale sun high up,
seen through a forest of very old trees.

It is light enough to see there is no way forward here.
Were you somehow to climb the steep cliffs,
there would only be a foreign land to traverse, perpetually.

This is the turning point
after the struggle of the underground journey.
It's time to go back now.

So you return through the tunnel,
passing the tableau of each room,
now the aching familiar.

And back through the gate,
up the long track and into the house
where the party you had left is still in progress.

It's a different time of day or season now.
Still the people play on,
oblivious to the alteration in you.

There is an imprint in your heart of the places you have been.
In future there will be no parties as such.
Some of the people will fade because that doesn't suit them.

You will want the house to be quieter.
You will remember that deep valley
with its old trees and far-away light.

You have come back above ground,
to home, to things that seem familiar,
but all is changed.

BIRDWORDS

Cockatoo Maths I

Cockatoos, in threes and fours
descend upon the flowering gum.
Then in fives and sixes
others come.
Until a long-division of large white birds
reduces the red blossom to equal shares.

Christmas Day on the Back Road to Clare – Trimming the Tree

On a hill-top the late afternoon sun
red-edges the leaves of a solitary tree,
and a festoon of sulphur-cresteds
string their flickering white candlepower throughout.

Cockatoo Cricket

Exclamations of cockatoos
land in the big Box Gum
until the dense green globe
is punctuated with white emphases.
Like a cricket match seen from high in the stand
with the last catch being noisily disputed.
Howzat!

Harvest Vestment

A rippling cloth across the orchard floor,
woven bright green warp, weft electric blue,
and all shot through with glistering red.
A brocade of rosellas works the windfall.

Cockatoo Law

A cross examination of cockatoos
interrogates the walnut tree.
Question mark crests rising in outrage
at the resistance.
Each shell is put to the question
until it cracks.

Zebs

The Zebra Finch No. 2 Aviary Band
practises the opening to Beethoven's fifth,
again and again.
And again.
Like all transcriptions to unlikely instruments
this sounds odd
and valiant at the same time.
But why should not small birds
aspire to greatness?

Sparrow Rugby

A scrum of small brown birds
locks onto the discarded breadcrust
and battles it up the path –
feathered hovercraft
with an erratic drive.
Until one escapes in possession
and lands triumphant in the end zone
thirty feet away between two birches.

Adelaide Tea Party

Black swans roost
on the banks of the Torrens,
a curious sculpture park
of fifty or more black sleeping teapots
with lowered neck loop handles
and wedgy tail spouts.

Crows

A smoke of crows climbs the thermals
at dusk, above the windbreak,
wheeling in, ballooning out.
In the trees below
flickering coals of rosellas settle for the night.

Dogfight

A squadron of finches
blurs in along the hedge,
then balls into a running battle down the side fence.
Sorties, furious cornerings in the bushes,
rapid fire chittering,
until the family dog
under a strafing of black and gold
streaks in full retreat to the verandah.

MISCHIEF

DIGGING UP THE FUTURE

Patient ID:80.176244
'a suspicious diffuse lucency in the left mandible'.

'Mandible' is a word used by people
who dig up long buried bones.
Archaeologists, palaeontologists
and forensic types who find truth
in tombs and mastodon graveyards,
and crime scenes.
Doctors too, but they abut it with words like
'lucent', a delicate and lovely word,
chunked with scientific exactitude
into telegraphic phrases that confound ordinary use.
Forget the face, the quiet smile.
Beneath it all she has mandibular lucency.

THE LIE

'Sir, would you by mistake have taken my book?
Packed it up at the end of class?
My name's on the inside.
Um … but, still, I thought, you know, I'd ask?'

He stills. Snaps: 'I would have noticed if I had.'
Moves just his eyes to watch her leave –
the tensile curve of spine, the swathe of hair,
the arc of her turning shoulder.

That night his fingers touch her name
inside the cover,
and all its youthful topography.

A BALLAD OF OFFICE POLITICS

In a small office somewhere
with a not-for-profit brief
public values hide
ambition's primal reach.

Two twenty-somethings stir
and think to show her out.
She's clearly old, past forty,
and really should depart.

They're tired of her directions
with which they don't agree,
any directions really,
and all the policies.

They don't perceive her teaching
of the bureaucratic maze,
her support through many errors
or the wisdom of her ways.

Knowing her strong ethic
of always prompt replies
Twenty-two cooks up an email storm,
laughs at the easy ride.

Twenty-three starts a new game next –
short chats only,
silence when she's walking past,
then full monosyllabary.

Week three they up the ante.
With others they confer
to youth-code speak the issues
and generally mis-tweet her.

The sage accountant visits,
dull bookkeeper that he is.
He scents the air and asks them
'I thought you were feminists?'

'Well yeeees' they say, impatient,
'but today there's so much more.
You have to break some eggs you know',
not knowing it for an old saw.

UNSTABLE PROJECTION

The still real, soon to be unreal outer world. The news not recalled on waking. Instead she enjoys the old reality still alive within this moment … until a pre-dawn jogger lopes past the side fence. The dotted line sound of mercurial feet a check to her own flat-lining. Running is a process, 'a condition of being carried forward'. Yesterday's news is an end, 'a limitation that indicates the full extent of a story'.

Then the knowledge begins to knock and tremble like a lantern caught in a storm. The shaking glass startles up shifting views. Then and then. Then and now. Now and next. On the outside it's logical enough, this dying business, but inside it feels strange. Disintegration from the known, a falling apart, a soon to be forever forgottenness. This morning is one of those pictures you can see in two ways. Or like the snow-globe when you shake it. Now you see it, now you don't. Tomorrow's waking will be more certain.

MAKING LAW

Basic Law: Israel as the Nation-State of the Jewish People.
19 July 2018

Girl-woman politician,
you've jammed the checklist
with military service, real-world work,
travel, marriage, children,
local cred,
and fluency in three languages.

At thirty-one you realised
your Knessett ambition.
Now you've made a law
erasing Arabic
as an official language.
Israel-born Arabs are now a special class of citizen.

And you've done this
Eighty years on from
the Citizenship Law, the Defence
of German Blood and Honour Law,
and the two thousand other Nuremberg Laws
for racial purity.

You may as well have dressed
in black precision,

spoken from a blank windowless edifice
designed to express mass
and power,
in Speer's mausoleum-like city

But you've done it
from the sunny courtyard
of a building designed for humanity
with warm colours,
light
and rounded corners,

Mistress of the walking shot,
you stare down the cameras,
'We are a right-wing government,
we're proud of it,
and we're bringing Israel
to a better place.'

You flirt with the camera like a light-thinking lass;
you are in fact made-over into volition.
Would-be sabra mane of wild hair,
useful in the activist stage,
now groomed to corporate dressing.
And with this vote you forget history.

OLD

CIRCLES

Yellow cup-and-saucer ride done,
my father looked over-long at the game of chance.
The showman's hand spun a round board through eight segments,
with state names, gaudy emblems.
Someone joked about Tasmania being the same size as the rest,
(no-one bothered with Canberra).
Quiet, he stepped up and put down two shillings.
Just like that.
Money was tight I knew, even at nine. Still more coins.
I had never seen this abandon in him, ever.
His face was somewhere else and I couldn't find him;
I worried for him but could not help.
More than a pound later we left. Empty-handed.
No talk on the walk home. I pretended this was normal.

The melanoid rubber bench is not high enough
for his old spine today.
So he drops the last distance as he sits,
and it jars him. Badly.
I need to watch that next time.
A hand-span's oval breadth, with a little point at the top,
A continent appears in blue marker on his shaved head.
'Might as well include Tasmania on the map eh?' the doctor says,
and loops his pen a little to the south-east.

A large round machine looms.
Quiet, he is lying down,
allowing the capsule to take him.
Giving himself up.
I worry for him, but cannot help.
His face is going to some other place
and I cannot reach him.

REMEMBRANCE DAY

The upper layer of earth in Flanders' Fields
has been ploughed so many times
few bones surface now.

The same with ancient places.
Experts need to dig deeply
to discern past lives.

The gone are overlaid by the present,
with 'good innings', 'duty done',
postage-stamp phrases to see them off.

Natural of course
but natural too is my wish not to forget
his hand harpooning a pickled onion in its jar;

the hailing host with a welcome for everyone,
the twinkling eyes knowing a weak pun
but offering it as an art form in itself;

the voice, the vigorous shuffle,
the murderous use of the walker
taking no prisoners of door frames.

AT 93

Ribbons of flight –
now he pilots a walking frame down the hallway.

The hurl of a motorbike –
handed in his driver's licence two years ago.

The shining rise of oars –
his arm shook lifting his coffee cup this morning.

Taught me the stars –
but cannot see far now,

and loved Tchaikovsky's music –
but cannot hear it these days.

He used to run punning riffs of words –
now his speech slurs in the nightly phone call.

The door to my father is closing.

OLD AGE

is his back screen-door closing in slow-motion
on its rusty spring.
Two quiet taps as it finds the jamb
recall the slap of summer thongs on bare heels.
The snick of the small lock
is a syncopated beat behind
long gone footsteps.

NOW-ISH

REPETITIONS

The crossword maker,
like a child with a new word,
uses 'davit' now.

Annoyingly,
it's hoisted almost daily.

RENOVATIONS

Young dreadlocked tilers
share their music liberally.
'1812' deep thumps,

in a different language,
but the same need for touching base.

DOVE

Hawk-hunted,
she meets plate-glass, and drops.
He soars off into the landscape,
the longer narrative of the living.

Here, the dove's fading orange feet
tremble three times,
nib-tipped toes reaching
to scribe a vanishing story.

A small life's undoing.
Fine brown back-feathers,
tiny fans with hearts of bronze,
and faint rims of old gold,
glint like guttering candles,
as the soft, scalloped cloak lifts and falls
around her shoulders
on the way to a still life.
Such a short story.

Gone now.
Twice her beak opened,
that gentle seed-hunting beak,
seeking breath, trying to speak,
before her head settled
in a small pool of blood.
Like an icon.
Or a small poem.

JUNE WEATHER

June 4

A wide pearl lid of low cloud
seals the valley.
Its flattening light dulls late autumn
to matte reds and yellow,
like tired old paint
soon to flake away.

June 5

My windscreen wipers have three modes
of discourse with the rain –
casual, regular, and manic.

A little elbow on the leftmost one
goes apoplectic at a downpour
and flings itself around in fury.

Like Mr Neill in Grade 4,
precipitated by the red-haired boy with a temper.

June 6

The sun hitches a ride north on the wind today.
It shoots a quick, reserved handshake into the bare trees,
where once it partied in full leaf.
It glances, short-tempered, off windows,
and proffers just a polite, cooling embrace to anyone looking
   for warmth.
It's getting out of town before the first big winter storm.

June 7

Lightning blades
cut the night.
Out of all proportion to the domestic streets below,
a dangerous stiletto-armed god strides the sky.

THE LITTLE YOSEI

A small boy hovers at the tram-stop.
He does not step beyond the circle
of his mother and sister.
He does not show off.
With Japanese formal manners intact
he quietly hops a faerie caper
to some music in his mind.

He's a metre tall
with a Mickey Mouse headdress.
The padded mask goes down to his eyes.
When looking from above
You see the famous mouse
until the child peers up at you.
Brown eyes shine, seeing more than this world.

He bird hops every third step of his dance.
'Yippee' he calls often,
and onto the tram he yips.
People smile and his mother quietens him,
although he is not seeking attention.
He still dances but in tiny jigs.
'Yippee' he whispers.

A glim of a boy is lighting the way.

To other seeing.

A small truth to hold out against a hard world.

[Yosei are benign Japanese fairies.]

THE AVENUE

It's Jacaranda season, a lilac-blue time
that escapes those driving down the nave
of the long blue cathedral, and the middle of their lives.

The shaded footpaths
are chapels of violet light.
When you walk there, they feel wide and high.

Blue expands the space around it,
and each tree in the avenue
is a blue mosque, a water-colour pavilion,

a purple tabernacle for seven weeks,
before the flowering eucalypts
and the heat of summer.

The ribs and arches of this ceiling
sing with eggshell blue
in the spell of early morning.

This is another world, insistent,
for those who are ready to see,
those with time and no pressing destination.

A straggling child gathers up five petal cups
and pieces them, with care, on a fence,
a tea-set in jacaranda blue.

An infant in the back seat of a passing car
looks up at the canopy. Stops crying.
His mouth and eyes widen.

Those who are old or unwell remember
flowers on a birthday dress, Chartres windows,
the gift of a blue glass jug, a jewel in a ring.

An elderly man walks over the lapis carpet
and quotes Exodus to himself, smiling,

> ... *a pavement made of sapphire stone,*
> *like the very heaven for its clearness ...*

Wakefield Press is an independent publishing and
distribution company based in Adelaide, South Australia.
We love good stories and publish beautiful books.
To see our full range of books, please visit our website at
www.wakefieldpress.com.au
where all titles are available for purchase.
To keep up with our latest releases, news and events,
subscribe to our monthly newsletter.

Find us!

Facebook: www.facebook.com/wakefield.press
Twitter: www.twitter.com/wakefieldpress
Instagram: www.instagram.com/wakefieldpress